WHISPERINGS
WITH LOVE
Thoughts, Words, Ideas
Are Ways to Happiness

Edward Kane, ACSW

Todd & Honeywell, Inc.
Great Neck, New York

Published by Todd & Honeywell, Inc.
          Ten Cuttermill Road
          Great Neck, New York 11021

ISBN 0-89962-316-6

Manufactured in the United States of America

To acknowledge all persons, personal
friends and associates who encouraged
me to put together the thoughts, words
and ideas as herein expressed. Several
secretaries who did the typing and
professional colleagues who gave me
various ideas which were embodied in
the material.
Jean McMackin, a professional artist,
is singled out for special thanks as
she supplied the illustrations.

To all who assisted me, my special
thanks.

The material contained in this book is
a cross section of thoughts, words and
ideas abstracted from my life's
experience as a psychotherapist, now
retired, and are expressions of my own
growth and development. These
pertain to the individual, as well as to
the interpersonal relationships of
couples, parents and children. It is
hoped that this will effect some
thoughtful reflections and meaningful
insights thus creating more productive
and satisfying life patterns.

Marriage
and
Married Couples

**The road least treaded
is the one to Fame.**

Share your treasure
by helping another
person to become
possessor of a
book you like.

When you want
something too
much the pursuit
will smother
the
accomplishment

Sex can help a married
couple in their emotional
maturing, providing positive
feelings are programmed
in the love making; otherwise
it is merely sex for sex sake.

Emotional security in marriage
is to have acceptance and
understanding; these being,
most important.

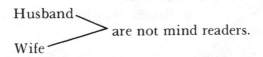

Husband
Wife
are not mind readers.

One big mistake in marriage
is that the wife fails to keep
herself a challenge to her
husband. Once he feels that
he has reached his goal, a
greater one must be replaced
in order to keep the challange
alive. Each day is a new day.

Marital roles reversed do
not insure security therein.

The remembering of birthdays
and holidays in marriage is
as important as showing
appropriate affection for
each other.

Whenever failure is experienced
in marriage, feelings of
success, importance, fulfillment
are sought outside.

It is a small man
    who strikes his wife.

There is need to accept marriage
with the vows you made; otherwise,
it will rock, and ultimately
      crumble.

Without ground rules,
      there is no marriage.

Tension in the marriage,
and the silent-treatment,
is like swinging a stick
at the beehive, and not
wanting to get stung.

Sometimes a wife cannot tell
her husband how she feels
about his mother, because he
is too emotionally involved with
her to permit this kind of
sharing of feelings.

Sex for sex sake keeps a
marriage glued together.
Intimacy in sexual relations
cements a marriage./
And the couple matures.

Changes in marital relations
are best tested by how they
feel.

Sex is not an absolute
ingredient for perpetuating
the marriage.
    The marriage can be
sustained through the positive
relationship which includes;
ground-rules by mutual
agreement.

In a relationship between
husband and wife, feelings
of importance have their
own pay-off.

In marriage, you cannot
expect to continue your
single life of the past.

Sex in Marriage

The body beautiful can be
appreciated and enjoyed;
but also needs to be respected.
However, the more you give of
feelings of self, the more you
shall receive in return.

Is your wife or husband a
'whipping-post' for your
insecurities?

There is frequently too much
sensitivity, concern, and
understanding with intimacy
before marriage.....once
married, too little!

Resolutions and Promises;
Communication stays alive
by daily, intimate talking.

When people feel praiseworthy
and secure in their goodness,
they do not need others to tell
them how good they are.

Whenever fears and inadequacies
are blown up out of proportion,
then the functioning level is less
than one's potential

The more positive our experiences,
    the more we mature.

Inadequacies are compensated
        over areas of human relations.

If you don't want to mess up—
        grow up.

To give freely of yourself
should have no strings attached
in order to be fully enjoyed.

Salt and pepper your life with
positive, meaningful experiences.
They are self-rewarding.

Interactions
should be positive and meaningful.

There should be more to your life
than beginning and ending with self.

If there is something wrong
with the relationship—
    look in the mirror.

There are just so many different
phases in the deck of life,
No more—No less; that is life.

The way you project your image
is not always the way others see you.

When emotions are in conflict communications break down.

Psychological Weight Reduction Formula :

When you program your life
around 'living' rather than
'eating', diet is simple.
The mind and energy is expended
on living; and then eating becomes
secondary. This principle is as
applicable as one's emotional
        maturity.

Too much intimacy frequently
causes people to take liberties
in saying and doing things which
can create hurt.
The rule is: intimacy is good,
but within limits.

A person's most important
life-line is that of feeling
needed.
This life-line is powerful,
tremendous and dynamic.

FEAR of how well you can make
        it as an adult...
FEAR of failing...
These serve as deterrents
        to success.

The more you put yourself to
any task, the more appreciation
is realized—from yourself,
from others, and from the
task itself.

Everyone has problems—answers
are in how one copes with the
pressures that created them
in the first place.

Love in a marriage is a state
of well-being which requires
many things, but most of all,
an intimate relationship.

Love is a state of being.
It is so broad that it has no
particular meaning in itself.

Love is a freedom to interact
without restraint in an
intimate relationship.

A person who is unemotional
triggers off, in the intimate
interaction with another,
harbored emotions in self-defense.

There is more that makes a
good marriage than relationships
and communications. It is the
christian spirit of the heart
that motivates the couple to an
inspearable union.

COURTSHIP: Too much sexual
             intimacy.

MARRIED: Frequently too
             little.

Our disappointments and
frustrations as well as
depressions can be
cushioned by having
faith that with an
improved attitude things
will get better for us.

Moral values can best
be understood when they are
discussed but not
criticized.

The most powerful and
meaningful communication
is that which is
experienced in
prayer.

As part of marriage, your
sex life is as individualistic
for you as the many aspects of
human behavior are tailored by
the individual.

A positive relationship
is most important in
marriage.

No wife should be
.   her husband's mop.

Loving intellectually
is not the same as
loving with touching,
hugging and feeling.

When we take too
much for granted
we are ill
prepared for eventualities.

Couples Planning Marriage

The power of a relationship
 is equal to that of love
in marriage.

Noting the difference in
people's beliefs and philo-
sophy, and being able to
relate to them is two different
things. The lack of understanding of this frequently causes
problems in the family and
in personal interactions.

Realization of ones problems
is the first step toward
acceptance which can then
lead to positive action in
solving problems!

Where there is compatability,
people can bridge their gap
of differences.

Being nice to each other,
doesn't mean you are happy.

When sex is used primarily
as a means of establishing
a relationship, this fact
can drive people further
away from having a relationship.

It is not how you love that
is important—but who you love.

A sound premarital relationship
obviates many conflicts in marriage.

When two people
compliment each other too
much, the relationship can
become stagnant.

Limiting the freedom of
   choice in a relationship
   causes frustration.

A good relationship can exist
between people without being
    intimate.

Relationship should be enriched
with time—if this is not
happening, there is something
wrong with the relationship.

Having all the satisfactions
and benefits of an uncommitted
relationship, without the benefit
of marriage, is realistically
non-fulfilling for lasting
    happiness.

Doing things that two people
enjoy together, does not,
of itself, mean there is a
relationship.

Excuses are not reasons.

Take one thing at a time and
proceed—allowing each situation
to be a stepping-stone to your
	success.

The more accurately you put
proper price-tags on behavior,
the better you can understand
	yourself.

It is not in the WHAT,
	but in the HOW
which perfects communications.

REFLECT!
Where have you been?
	Where are you now?
		Where are you going?

You can never make out
	by running.

Dimensions you can handle.
    Intentions are the problem.

Anything
done in excess
is destructive.

When not sure—
say nothing.

Irritation with self
    may be projected on to others.

If that's what you are looking
for, that's what you will find.

A
MEMORY FOREVER:
Once said, it cannot be erased.

Indifference breeds rejection.

React to a situation as it is,
and not as it appears.

Secrets
are normal with intimacy.

The need to escape
is ever present in all of us.

It takes more than thinking
to make things happen.

Whenever your feelings about
yourself are not great,
then you cannot accept compliments
for what they are.

To love is to give freely,
    and not be possessive.

All kinds of communication
does not make for understanding.

Truth needs no support.
    It stands alone.

A Thought kept alive
cannot be set aside

Blame is frequently a projection
and a cover-up for the real
thing. Accepting this "hot
potato" can frequently burn
a hole in the marriage contract.

Stubborness serves no real purpose.

A good insurance against being
hurt when people strike out
is to depersonalize the comment.

Everything in moderation is good.
   Anything in excess is bad.

Self-image is as important to
the personality as eating and
sleeping. All are equally
necessary for a productive
      life.

Regarding the hurts...
consider the source and adjust
the response accordingly.

PROMISES:
Only as good as they are kept.

If you can't help someone,
    do nothing to hurt him.

Appreciation is as integral to love
as the fingers are to the hand.

**To give completely of yourself
is beautiful.**

The most dynamic thread of life
is the fine line separation:

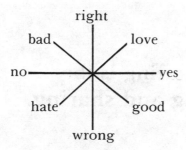

Live and let live in a way
that your convictions are not
a deterrent to your happiness.

Anything that affects life
    in a positive way
        is therapeutic.

RESPECT is not obtained by a
single act. It is an accumulated
growth process, stemming from one's
own feeling of security and self-
confidence, plus ability to make
proper decisions.

SEX is not necessary for a
    heterosexual relationship.

**True caring is the
giving and sharing.**

Healthy dependency, other than
meeting basic needs in sharing
and giving to one another,
promotes intimacy, emotional
growth, and affection, this
is self-rewarding and self-
perpetuating. The converse
    is destruction.

PARENTS

and

CHILDREN

To give of self and to share,
is a major requirement for a
successful marriage. Being
able to divide yourself and
balance the scales with the
child by giving affection and
attention, is truly a delicate
process; and more so, when
there is more than one child.

Whenever the parent overidentifies
with the child's behavior, and
sees in the child some part of
their own behavior, making the
right decision on the child's
behalf is very difficult.

Early corrective measures
regarding your child's handicap—
with a parents' healthy attitude—
will do much to aid the child's
adjustmet and/or recovery.

When parents relate to children
believing they are as mature
as themselves, this can create
          problems

When parents are one step ahead
of the child, many problems
can be avoided.

Children have their
most normal growth
in a positive,
permissive, and
structured emotional
climate.

Children who are
emotionally immature, will not
understand more than their
maturity will permit.

A child inhibited
will relate in accordance with
his inhibitions.

Children ask 'dumb' questions,
but parents improperly label
        them.

Parents who over-react to their
child's behavior frequently impose
punishment disproportionate to
infraction of the rules.

A mother, saying to a child,
"Don't steal", is not what
will stop him from stealing.
Saying something does not make
        it so.

        The nature of the
emotional climate in the home aids
family emotional growth.

If children are used by parents
they will be abused, and ultimately
will retaliate.

Restrictions:
should be geared to the offense
and not as punishment for
punishment's sake.

When parents rebel against their
children's rebellious behavior,
they make it more difficult
for the child to calm down.

One of the greatest contributing
factors to children's problems is
parental lack of agreement as to
how discipline should be enacted.

Children's ability to adjust
to change is directly related
to the emotional security
their parents project.

The greatest contribution to
the building of a child's
character is to give him
responsibility he can handle.

An established routine for
children enhances maturing.

The first born baby is
        the intruder to the
        parents intimacy,
And, frequently, has to pay a
        price for being Number one.
Hence, parents need to share
each other with the child for
the good of everyone.

Children should not be given
more responsibility than they
are able to handle, such as
having to make adult decisions.

When the emotional needs of
a child are not being met,
the child will resort to activities
not acceptable to parents: such
as; taking money to have a
love-need fulfulled.

Family life is as strong as
    parents interact with one
        another and with children.

A child will divide and conquer
as long as there is a double-
standard for discipline.

Mothers who get away from their
children from time to time
are helped, thereby, to be better
mothers and see their children
as more loving.

Parents who relate to children,
believing because they use the
same words as adults they are
understood, can expect
        some misunderstanding.

Parents should not criticize
one another in front of their
        child.

Children learn early how to
play parents against one another
for their own gains.
Parents who are unable to control
their own childhood feelings
get caught in the middle.

Parents need to realize that
standards set for their children
are not necessarily acceptable
to other parents. If there is
any kind of understanding between
sets of parents, it is important
that each other's standards are
respected for what they are.

When parents are frustrated
        with each other,
They may take out their frustrations
        on the children.

The more you are in tune with
your own emotional needs, then
those of your children can be
better recognized for what
they are instead of how they
      appear.

Do not allow domination and
overpowering to be the major
ground-rule in your relationship.
This can be destructive.

Parents frequently saddle
children with responsibility
far ahead of their capacity
for fulfillment.

Whatever sacrifices parents make
on behalf of their children,
they reap rewards far beyond
      description.

A man's level of functioning has
an infinitesimal capacity for
      expression.

Parents frequently want children
to turn 180 degrees in their
behavior so as to relieve
their guilt for what they have
done to cause the problems
which the children have.

For the children who are
uninhibited, they express their
feelings freely.
The adult is inhibited and his free
association of ideas is extremely
difficult because of the defenses,
inhibitions, anxieties, frustrations.
fears, etc.

If you are not one step ahead
of your child, you are one step
        behind.

It is not the spoken word that
is important...it is the way
        the word is spoken.

Dependency beyond necessity
retards emotional growth and
is destructive to a relationship.

A child's success or failure
in getting along outside the
home, is directly related to
how well he gets along at
        home.

In the absence of the father,
the mother keeps the father's
image alive in the home.
This is related to the relationship they have with one another.
Of course, the reverse is also
        true.

A rule of the thumb,
particularly for
children, is if you
don't want to lend
your possessions
then don't borrow.

The more you are in
touch with your
feelings and love
yourself, the more
you can relate to
others.

Children enjoy freedom
and all the privileges
it gives however they
must equally accept
and respect authority.

GOD IS GOOD

Faith in yourself
is directly related
to the faith you
have in God.

There is nothing wrong
about being childlike
in your relationship
with God. The more you
are, the more you will
experience His love
and be happy.

When you are completely at
loss to find a solution to
your problems, turn them
over to God and the faith you
have will give you the best
solution but not necessarily
the one you are seeking.

At a time of crisis or at
any other time of need
when an easy solution is
not at hand pray and
ask for guidance to a
satisfactory thoughtful
resolution of your problem.

"GEMS"
FOR
THOUGHT

Positive experiences
are insurance against depression.

Your acceptance by people is
not contingent on the giving
of material things, but how
well you have accepted yourself
and project this image.

Happiness is more
assured when there
is greater emotional
control, self discipline
and consistency.

Sympathy
is no substitute for empathy.

The more good deeds we perform
the better we feel, and the
self-image is enhanced.

Do not vegetate—
LIVE life.

Say what you meam.
  Mean what you say.
    Be consistent.

Knowing it
  Believing it
    Accepting it
Knowing something is not enough.
You need to Believe it and Accept
it. Then you can put the idea
into use. This is especially
difficult for youth to do for
they feel that knowing so many
different things makes them adults.

Feelings of unworthiness are
directly linked to our failures or
lack of successes.

          TALK,
and you become more aware of
 your situations and solutions.

Fulfillment is not satisfied
by material things.

Out of good, comes good.

Concern is to life
  as painful suffering is to death.

'Accidentally on purpose' has
more meaning to it than meets
the eye. People fall, drop
things, bump into one another,
have car accidents when pre-
occupied and disturbed. There
is more to this behavior than
meets the eye.

The fact that you don't remember
having said something, doesn't
mean that you had not said it.

The hope is for the pieces
to fall into place before you
fall to pieces.

Retaliatory behavior is expressed
not merely in the here-and-now
but to encounters of another
        time.

The very things you try to
prevent will cause them,
expecially when you are
frustrated.

When you have nothing to look
forward to, then there is nothing
else to do but to look back on
the past. This tends to age
people without their realizing it.

Sitting in judgment of self,
is similar to doing things
to others as they were done
to you.

In order to effect any change
of self, this is predicated
        on 'wanting'.

Where there is demanding, there
   cannot be true giving.

Inconsistency is:
   getting nowhere.

The more you can identify the
problem for what it is, the
better you can understand it
   and help yourself.

Emotional tones are like octaves
of the musical scale. When
people don't get the reassurance
they need, they become depressed
and/or hostile.

Whenever you have a complex
problem, it is best to first
baste it, in order to see if
it fits, before you attempt
to sew it together.

To fantasize
costs nothing,
but
can be costly.

What you feel and touch is not
quite the same as what you
touch and feel.

A negative attitude
is a road-block to happiness.

Life is a continuous process.
It is like time—it never stops.

Fame and fortune has a way
of decapitating man by his
    own hand.

Half the fun in life
    is wishing and expecting.
Once realized, it is not fulfilling.

Man's use of the power of
    suggestion,
is as effective as man's use of
    self.

Time places limits on man
and has unlimited striking
    minutes.

Frequently **APPEARANCE** makes
a beautiful presentation of
    what we are not.

What constitutes acceptance for you?

In adult life, when the need
is greater to act like a child,
then growing offers little reward.

Living in the past,
to the exclusion of the present,
is non-productive.

Ask yourself from time to
time, "What am I trying to
prove by my behavior?" The
answers you get may be surprising.

Too much repetition and monotony
frequently leads to life boredom.

Not being able to live in the
past, and at the same time in
the present, causes an emotional
stalemate—lethargy and immobility.

**Day is continuous
only separated by night.**

When emotions overtake the
ideas that are being expressed,
there is very little understanding.

Finding one's self in the
attainment of happiness,
is, for some, as important as
the need to sew.

Anyone who goes to extremes
to prove a point,
proves he needed extremes
to do it.

The road best traveled
is the one to heaven.

Christian Love is
magnificently
expressed when you
can make an angered
person smile and
feel your love.